WHERE DO ANIMALS POOP?

WHERE DO ANIMALS POOP?

a sequel to
What Do Animals Eat?

A

B

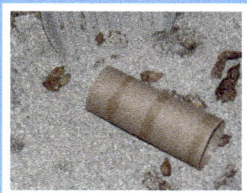

C

Written by **BONNIE BANKS-BEERS**

Photography by **BONNIE BANKS-BEERS** and
SARAH A. BEERS

EPIGRAPH BOOKS
RHINEBECK, NEW YORK

Where Do Animals Poop? © 2018 by Bonnie Banks-Beers

ISBN: 978-1-948796-34-7

Library of Congress Control Number: 2018955339

Book design by Colin Rolfe

Epigraph Books
22 East Market Street, Suite 304
Rhinebeck, NY 12572
(845) 876-4861
Epigraphps.com

"As the whole world is a school for the human race...
so every individual's lifetime is a school
from the cradle to the grave."

—JOHN AMOS COMENIUS

DEDICATION

To the students of
Saucon Valley Elementary School:

I remember when
I was your age and was once one of you.

ACKNOWLEDGMENTS

I'd like to give a general acknowledgment to all who contributed to this book through providing photo opportunities. (See "Poop Picture Sources" page for a complete listing.)

Specifically, I'd like to acknowledge:

Pete Fox, VP of Marketing and Operations, Lehigh Valley Zoo, for his openness to my book idea and for allowing us a bit of behind-the-scenes zoo access during the zoo's busy pre-holiday time,

and

Chris Sauder, Animal Care, Lehigh Valley Zoo, who was an amazingly big help accompanying us around the zoo so we could view and photograph the poops of 10 different animals. Chris was a very efficient and knowledgeable guide who carved out time in his schedule to make sure we could take the pictures we needed, and even collected cockatoo and skunk poop in advance of our last zoo visit to help expedite the process.

Thanks also to Molly, who continually asked me, "Is the sequel finished yet?" as the writing process for this book took longer than I anticipated. Her pointed questioning helped keep me on track, working toward completing my goal.

Big thanks to my family for joining me on some unusual expeditions, all in the name of animal research.

And thanks, of course, to Jonah, who not only initiated (and illustrated) the first book of this series, but also composed the opening stanza to this book.

Special thanks to Paul and Colin at Epigraph Publishing Services for all of their hard work, patience, and willingness to put together a sequel comparable to the original.

WHERE DO ANIMALS POOP?

(A Sequel to *What Do Animals Eat?*)

Where Do Animals POOP?
    Let's go find out, let's go snoop.
When you're outside, look at the ground.
    As a matter of fact, take a look all around!

When you're outside on a walk,
    you may see an animal or its footprints
or maybe just POOP left behind:
    the animal's identity left as a hint.

Gardens, lawns with healthy soil
    contain roots where earthworms live.
Surfacing in wet spring or fall,
    WORM CASTINGS (worm POOP) they give.

Just like animals move
    in water or land or sky,
they also make MOVEMENTS
    as they swim or walk or fly.

    Now as you page through this book
    look at the HIGHLIGHTED WORDS:
POOP and fifty-two synonyms
    that function as nouns or as verbs.

AMERICAN ALLIGATORS

Alligators like to POOP wherever they feel the urge to GO.
　　It's the same way with some snakes and sharks
　　and whales and moose, you know.
Some animals POOP in a special place to mark their territory,
　　but alligators POOP when they are eating,
　　to make digestive space free.

Their STOOLS are similar to those of birds,
part whitish and part brownish-green,
　　eliminated through a cloaca
　　(a "common sewer", it means).
While people have a hole for pee and a separate hole for POO,
　　the alligator has only one hole (like other reptiles do).

"COPROLITES" are "POOP fossils". Now there's a term to know!
　　Some were made by ancestors of alligators long ago.
Scientists can find, collect, and study such fossilized DUNG
　　that came from prehistoric swamps
　　where earlier life had begun.

Bats

GUANO is DUNG that's from bats or seabirds.
  On islands of Peru they came up with this word.
It's a good fertilizer that helps crops to grow
  healthy flowers or fruits when organic farmers sow.

Bats sleep upside down, often in caves and trees,
  and even can POOP upside down, if they please!
Some bats eat fruit and then POOP out the seeds,
  planting new plants while flying—yes, indeed.

Bats, eating insects, make sparkly POO.
  Because they eat insects, here's just what they do:
They chew them up finely, exoskeletons and all,
  then POOP out the sparkly tubes, dark brown and small.

People build birdhouses to attract birds,
  often to watch them and listen (observe);
people build bat houses to attract bats,
  for they eat mosquitoes. How helpful is that!

Bats, as we know, like to come out at night.
  In daytime they sleep, squeezed in places quite tight.
So if you have a bat house, or know where they dwell,
  just look down below and see where GUANO fell.

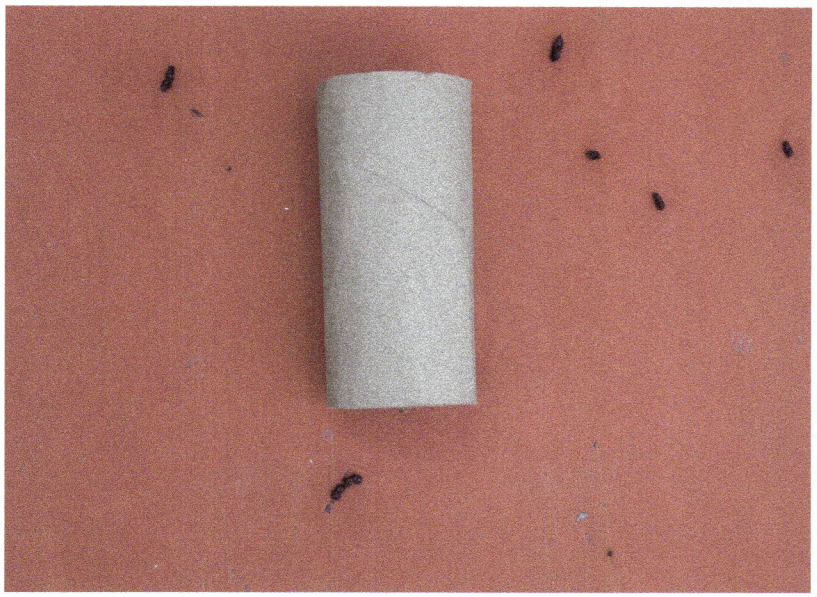

Cats

Big cats in the wild (lions, tigers, and more)
    mark their territory, for they're living outdoors.
Small wild cats have to bury their POO
    to hide from their predators and protect kittens, too.

Domestic cats share the small wild cats' trait:
    in litter boxes or gardens, they bury their WASTE.
It's a natural instinct for small felines world-round
    to dispose of their FECES, away underground.

Cat POOP can be smelly and dirty with germs.
    Outdoors, feral cats pick up parasites, worms.
Remember to wash hands (if a cat is your pet),
    after scooping up POOP, so clean hands you will get.

Now here's something odd: the Indonesian "toddy cat"
    helps make pricey "civet coffee". How does it do that?
It climbs coffee trees, eats ripe "cherries", and POOS
    out the pits (coffee beans!) to be cleaned, roasted, brewed.

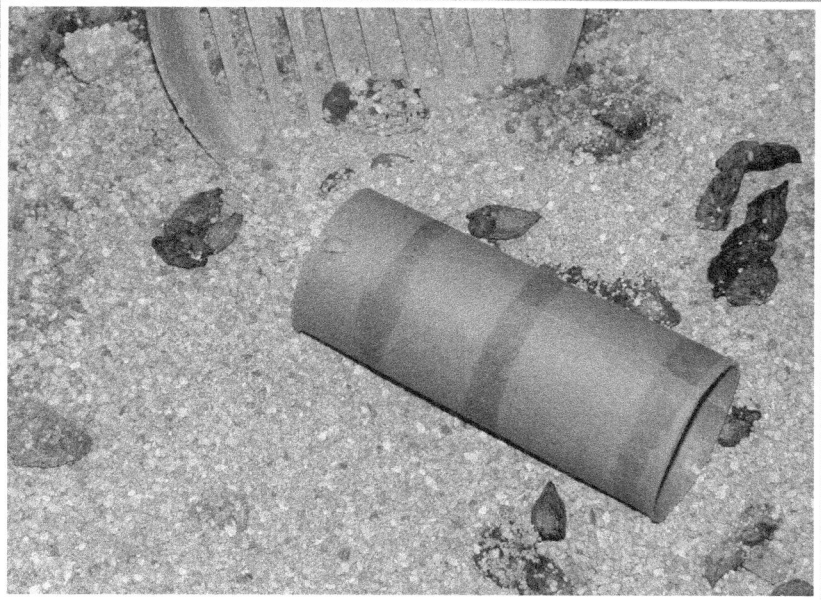

Dogs

Dogs sometimes POOP in their owner's backyard
   if they're trained to go there (some folks say it's not hard).
Dogs POOP where they play, too, like in a dog park.
   So please "clean up after" when out for a walk.

Quite often you see a dog pee on a tree—
   it's their way of marking their territory.
Since some dogs seem to go POOP wherever they choose,
   watch out on the sidewalk, it messes your shoes!

Have you watched a dog, outside, look for "the right spot"?
   He sniffs, and he searches—will he POOP there or not?
Some scientists, researching where dogs go "NUMBER TWO",
   observed magnetic fields where dogs make their DOO-DOO.

When DOG DIRT is left outside to decompose,
   who should come sniffing about with their nose?
Rats and mice. They eat dog FECES to glean
   bits of undigested food; they help to clean.

ELEPHANTS

Elephants are the largest animals
who live upon land, not sea.
    They have voracious appetites and make
    POOP piles quite grand to see.
A 20-pound pile they make once in a while
(and every few hours to "GO" is their style),
    from digested grass and leaves and fruit…
    plus gallons and gallons of pee!

On average an African elephant eats
300 pounds per day,
    producing over 150 pounds
    of POOP along the way!
Each POOP BALL is almost two pounds in weight,
and almost 100 per day is the rate
    of how many an elephant DROPS as s/he
    walks along the way.

Its fibery DUNG creates a home
for crickets and scorpions, too.
    Who'd've thought that such critters
    could live in a pile of POO?
Monkeys, birds, meerkats all forage for food
in elephant DUNG—its beetles taste good!
    And Thai people pick out PASSED coffee beans
    for "Black Ivory Coffee" to brew.

If left upon the ground, the POOP
will help to plant fruit trees
    if the elephant ate "elephant apples" or guava,
    and then POOPED out the seeds.
If folks collect elephant DUNG (they do!),
they can make a recycled paper (it's true!)…
    Or burn BM's for mosquito repellent…
    or ferment FECES for fuel—yes, indeed!

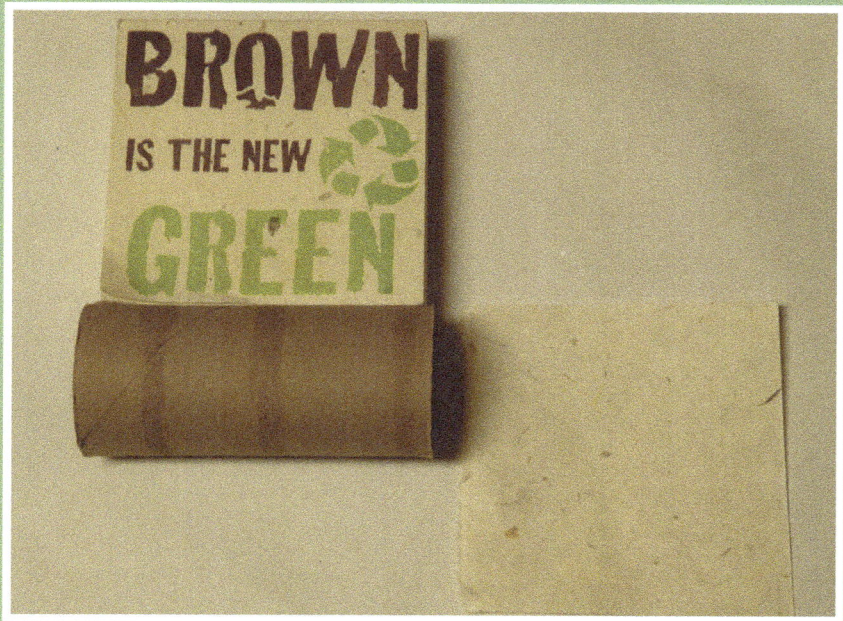

FISH

Some fish in the wild do what elephants do:
 they eat lots of seeds, then plant trees with their POO.
The Amazon "tambaqui" eats many fruit seeds
 that fall in the water, then plant trees with FECES.

There are 7 quintillion, 500 quadrillion (in the world)
grains of sand.
 Would you believe some's parrotfish POOP,
 making Hawaii's white beaches quite grand?
They scrape and they bite, from morning 'til night—
coral reef algae they like to eat.
 As their teeth break down coral to a sand, finely ground,
 their intestines a "SAND CLOUD" EXCRETE.

Near the Bahama's tropical beaches there are muddy sea floors
 that are made up of coral and shells, and even more.
This calcium carbonate "MARINE MUD" sediment
 is comprised of fish POOP—about 14%.

"Spotted SCAT" —popular aquarium pets—
 are silver with brown spots, a squared fish that gets
its name from said habit of eating FECES
 in brackish (briny) water, often Japanese.

No matter where fish live, most have one thing in common
    (except bony fish like sunfish, groupers, and marlin):
they have a cloaca—one hole like reptiles and birds.
    Why, even sharks eliminate pee that's mixed with TURDS.

GEESE

A typical goose POOPS a lot in one day:
    two dozen or more times is what experts say.
The DROPPINGS look more like a dog's than a bird's.
    'Round many a lake you'll spy black and white TURDS.

They POOP while they're grazing or walking around,
    thus, most of their POOP can be found on the ground.
They POOP right before take-off to fly, it is told;
    they empty cloacas to lighten their load.

Now here's "the POOP", or what to know:
    in ponds, it makes the algae grow,
on grass (if it's touched), it can cause bad diseases.
    So please do not touch any FECES from geeses…

Unless, of course, you are trained what to do,
    like making a compost of leaves and goose POO
or converting goose DROPPINGS into pellets that could
    be burned in wood stoves somewhat faster than wood.

Horses

"Horse MANURE" is an expression that means
    "what a pile of nonsense!"
Horse MANURE is also DUNG
    that emits earthy pungence.

If an apple a day keeps the doctor away,
    then what does a "ROAD APPLE" do?
It sits in the road where the horse did unload
    this apple-shaped slang for horse POO.

Grass and hay and grain and treats
and lots of water, too
    help make a happy, healthy horse
    and piles of healthy POO.
They say the average horse can POOP
nigh 50 pounds per day,
    in one year's time about nine tons—so fertilize away!

In fact, there are some specialized farmers
    who put horse MANURE in darkened rooms,
and mix a very moist and rich soil
    to grow tasty fungi called mushrooms.

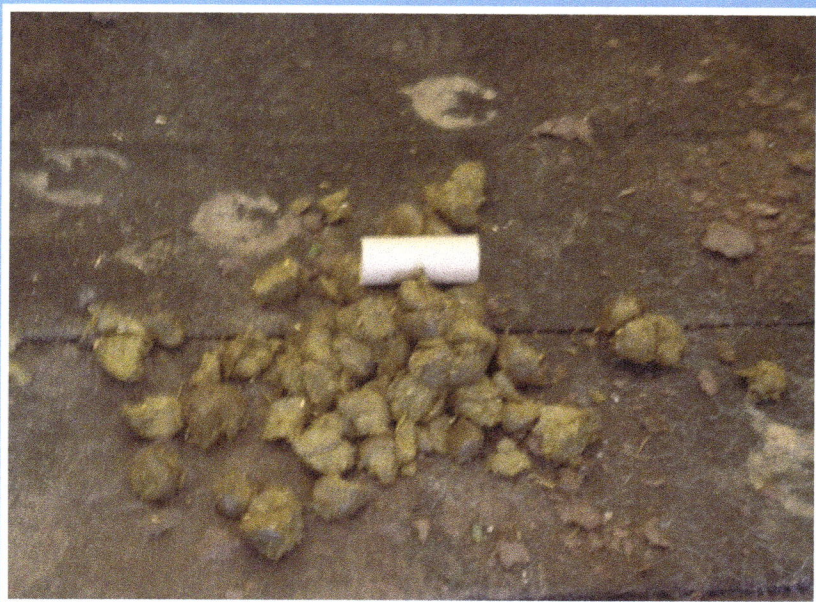

INSECTS

While Thai folks use elephant POOP
to make "Black Ivory Coffee",
    the Chinese brew moth caterpillar POOP
    to make a fragrant black tea.
"Chong Shi Cha", or "Worm DROPPING Tea",
is said to taste like mint,
    cool you down on a summer day,
    and brew to a reddish-brown tint.

Land insects do not urinate—
conserving water's what they do.
    They make a dry waste called "FRASS"—
    it is the insects' type of POO.
Insects that live in water make
a FRASS that's more like pee.
    Perhaps because they're surrounded by water,
    their frass is more soggy!

Ants get nutrients from bird DROPPINGS,
    and flies get energy to fly
from eating POOP they land upon.
    It's strange; I wonder why.

With so many animals alive in the world,
why isn't there POOP everywhere?
    The answer is varied, and complex for sure,
    but of one fact you ought be aware:

an insect that's called the "DUNG beetle" does
the job of a strong trash collector.
   They tunnel POOP or often roll it in balls,
   to be dinner or egg incubators.

DUNG beetles roll deer POOP in Florida;
   in the Amazon rainforest, monkey DROPPINGS;
the buffalo DUNG's rolled in Africa;
   in Australia they roll kangaroo PLOPPINGS.

As a matter of fact, on six continents,
   the DUNG beetle does reside.
It has been estimated that
   there are 6,000 species worldwide!

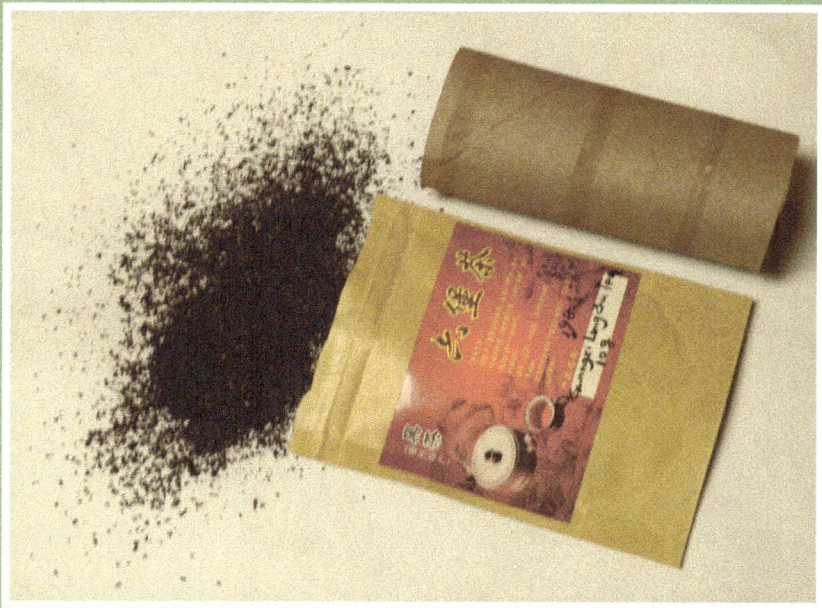

JERSEY COWS

Cow MANURE, dried, mixed with dirt,
can help food crops to grow.
    This is quite a useful tip
    that vegetable farmers know.
In fact, fermented "cow PATTIES"
can produce methane gas
    which can make electricity—
    now how useful is that!

In Wisconsin, when folks aren't
too busy making cheese
    they have "cow CHIP" tossing contests—
    dried DUNG's tossed like frisbees.
The distance that's on record is 185 feet,
    or more than half a football field—
    now that is quite a feat!

In Africa, the "cow PIES" are
not just for fun and games.
    These fibrous FLOPS can heat a home
    when ignited with flames.
And East African huts can become waterproofed faster
    when they have sticks and grass coated
    with some "cow DUNG plaster".

You see, the FECES of a cow, a bovine animal,
has lots of synonyms that can be kind of laughable.
You may have noticed that some terms
are also types of food:
"cow PATTIES", "CHIPS", and "PIES"—
and "MEADOW MUFFINS", to include.

KANGAROOS

Native to Australia are animals who, like cattle, eat grass,
    and when they have to "GO TO THE LOO",
    some fibery brown PELLETS they PASS.
This kangaroo SCAT is collected by some
to make garden compost (to grow food),
    and gathered by others instead of kindling
    for tinder (to light firewood).

When early European explorers saw
the kangaroo for the very first time,
    they saw an animal who, to them,
    had really no reason or rhyme.
With a head like a deer, standing up like a man,
and like a frog hopping around,
    this newly found beast sometimes seemed two-headed
    when a baby in its pouch was found.

As you may know, it's about nine months
that a human baby develops in a womb;
    but did you know it's close to only one month
    for a baby kangaroo?
As long as a jellybean, from head to toe,
it climbs at birth and then it goes
    into the mother kangaroo's pouch
    to eat and sleep and grow.

And just like baby people who,
after eating, pee and POO,
    it is the same way for a "joey",
    or a baby kangaroo.
Because inside the mother's pouch
no diaper can e'er be seen,
    her long tongue comes out (from her long snout)
    to lick pouch crevices clean.

For almost a year,
    while the joey lives here,
the mom's like a deer,
    and licks its bottom clear!

In fact, there're lots of parents in
the animal kingdom, worldwide,
    who rid their pouches or their nests
    of FECES, to clean inside.
Some baby birds, like robins, poop
in mucousy "FECAL SACS"
    that parents eat or carry away
    like disposable diaper packs.

23

LIONHEAD RABBITS

Rabbits outside POOP on
grass, ground, or snow;
    rabbits inside have their own place to GO.
They say you can house-train a bunny as a pet:
    its own bunny potty you may want to get!

You'll notice there're two kinds of
DROPPINGS from bunnies,
    both from the same rabbit—
    I know this sounds funny.
Their more common POOP is the size of a pea:
    200 per day, and quite dry and grassy.

Their less common POOP is called a "CECOTROPE".
    Its healthy bacteria help bunnies to cope.
They resemble brown mulberries, coated with mucus.
    Bunnies often eat these "NIGHT DROPPINGS"
    as they exit the anus.

Mice

Mice live in most countries,
burrowing underground.
    Sometimes inside buildings
    and houses they're found.
They sleep during the day and
then come out at night,
    these omnivorous beasts with
    voracious appetites.

They POOP near their food source,
often near their nest.
    Loving crackers and cereal,
    they chew cardboard best.
Don't eat food they've contaminated—
you have been warned.
    Don't touch DROPPINGS; don't sweep
    (it sends germs airborne).

One mouse can POOP 50+ PELLETS per day.
    These MOVEMENTS look like dark rice
    or brown caraway,
with 30+ diseases that folks can get.
    Get rid of indoor rodents,
    unless they're your pets!

NUBIAN GOATS

Baby goats and little folks are
both called "kids", you may know.
    As mammals, they share common traits
    when born and as they grow:
a backbone, hair, and breathing air,
and drinking milk when young.
    These warm-blooded animals, too,
    have similar baby DUNG.

The earliest STOOL of a mammal baby
    is thick, greenish-black, and can be quite sticky.
"MECONIUM" is what this newborn POOP's called
    for goats or for humans. Now don't be appalled

to find out POOP traits infant mammals can share.
    Both kids (baby goats and humans) —be aware—
when drinking mothers' milk,
have FECES' color change
    to mustardy yellow. So do not think it strange

to find out when goats next eat solids, like hay,
    the yellowish color no longer will stay.
It's brown, like solid-eating humans' appears,
    but formed in small PELLETS,
    like rabbits' and deer's.

In semi-deserts of Morocco, a common sight is seen:
 goats climb up (high!) in argan trees
 to graze upon fruit and leaves.
And then they EXCRETE argan seeds
(which they cannot digest)
 that can be gathered to make oil
 by an age-old process.

OSTRICHES

We have learned that the gator and the goose
    have one hole for pee and POO to vamoose.
Excreting urine and FECES together,
    both gators and geese are "birds of a feather".

In fact, their hole for pee and POO
    is the same hole that lays eggs, too.
In birds it is quite often known as the vent,
    same name as the top of a volcano's ascent.

Ostriches have this cloaca, or vent,
    this hole where their WASTE matter's naturally sent.
While other birds have DROPPINGS
(EXCREMENT, urine) combined,
    ostriches go "number one"
    and "NUMBER TWO" from behind.

Since ostriches are birds that aren't built to fly,
    their DROPPINGS won't fall on you, down from the sky.
Ostriches also lay eggs from this hole—
    the largest bird eggs in the world, don't you know!

Penguins

GUANO is the DUNG of seabirds and bats.
    Remember, Peru's where they came up with that
name for this plant-helping fertile MANURE
    that seabirds and bats make, and farmers procure.

Penguin POOP helps many plants to grow strong,
    and protects unhatched chicks. Their life is prolonged
when ground-nesting penguins spray "POOP RINGS" around
    their nests to keep harmful insects out of bounds.

They stand on the edge of their nests, forward bending,
    lift tails and squirt POOP out—quickly projecting
it about 40 centimeters away
    (about 16 inches), for that is their way.

In fact, before even beginning to build
    their nests, they clear space that originally was filled
with snow and ice by melting it with—yes—POOP.
    They don't need a shovel, they don't have to scoop!

What color is GUANO from these penguins black and white?
    It depends upon their diet and their appetite.
From feasting on some squid their POOP can come out
brown or yellow,
    while eating fish makes it turn gray or white—
    a bit more mellow.

If dining on algae, their POOP becomes green—
    this can occur if food sources are lean.
A common (from eating krill) color is pink.
    Now all of these colors can make someone think

that it's not too odd when some space satellites
    spot penguin POOP colors against the white ice.
These pictures tell scientists where penguins live.
    What information penguin GUANO can give!

QUAILS

"On the first day of Christmas my true love gave to me
 a partri-idge in a pear tree." That's rare to see!
The ground-nesting partridge, like a turkey, fans its tail.
 Both are members of the same family as the quail.

Quail like to eat mostly insects, plants, and seeds.
 And like other birds, they've a cloaca for FECES.
"Backyard chickens" (quail) sometimes live inside a coop.
 Their baby chicks may walk backwards
 when they have to POOP!

Quail farmers like the MANURE—it's called "BROWN GOLD".
 So do some jewelry makers. Here's what I've been told:
The "MANURE Man of South Carolina" made
quail-DROPPING jewelry
 and talked about it on the *Tonight Show*,
 where he became a celebrity.

RED-TAILED HAWKS

Red-tailed hawks are country birds and city birds as well.
    Did you know in Central Park
    some red-tailed hawks do dwell?
There these city birds can prey upon squirrels, pigeons, rats.
    But unlike quail, who POOP below,
    hawks go up to make SCAT.

Typically, they DEFECATE while high up in a tree,
    sitting on a perch (a branch),
    and this is what you'd see:
hawk bends over, lifts its tail, and then gives quite a push,
    squirting a long strand of SCAT that
    travels quite fast—whoosh!

When the hawk's done making POOP—
or "SLICING", 'tis the word—
    it will flick its tail feathers (no T.P. for birds!).
When the WASTE lands on the ground
or elsewhere (the sidewalk?),
    since its color's mainly white
    it's sometimes called "HAWK CHALK".

"HAWK CHALK", although mostly white,
is also black and green.
    Uric acid crystals give this SPLAT its whitish sheen.
Some green streaks (from bile that was used to digest fat)
    and black streaks (remnants of meals)
    make colorful hawk SCAT.

Even much more colorful than
green-black-white hawk SCAT
    is something that's called "lichen"—
    looks like a slow-growing plant.
Beneath perches of birds (like hawks),
these algae-fungi slowly grow on trees
    and rocks, absorbing nitrogen
    from SCAT to branch out brilliantly.

So many animals begin with S
(and end with an S, it is true).
Let's take a look at a smattering of them
and learn some things about their POO.

Skunks

Dogs DEFECATE with some "anal sac fluid"
    to help mark their territory;
skunks spray their smelly secretions when they're scared
    to protect themselves naturally.

Skunks are omnivorous: both plants and animals
    are what these "night owls" do eat.
Their POOP looks like mushy feline FECES, and it can
    contain fur, feathers, and seeds.

Sloths

In rainforest canopies of South America,
    sloths hang upside down from cecropia trees.
These "folivores" eat mostly leaves, at night (or twilight),
    and sleep lots of hours each day—10 to 20!

Once per week, with a belly like St. Nick's,
    they slowly descend from their tree,
DEFECATE on the ground, perhaps cover their WASTE,
    then slowly ascend, more skinny.

Snakes

Snakes are reptiles, with cloaca, whose TURDS
    are often mistaken for lizards' or birds'.
Some snakes rattle or hiss—a defensive art;
    the coral snake's known to make "defensive farts".

Snakes eat a meal once every few days
    or sometimes once every couple of weeks.
With that same frequency, they make MOVEMENTS.
    E'en far less often can be their technique.

SQUIRRELS

Squirrel POOP looks like rats' (but more fat):
    it is tubular and shades of brown.
Because they POO "on the run", piles
    do not accumulate on the ground.

Neither does their babies' POOP pile up
    when they're defenseless, at home in their nest.
Mother squirrels lick the babies' bottoms (like deer)
    and carry POOP away by mouth. It disappears!

So many synonyms for the word POOP
begin with S, by the way:
SAND CLOUD, SCAT, SLICE, SOIL, SPLAT,
SPRAINT, *and* STOOLS,
as well as SPLATTER *and* SPLAY.

Storks

People, when they're feeling hot, quite often tend to sweat.
    And as the sweat evaporates, the more cooled off they get.
Dogs often pant—and birds can, too—to cool off in the heat.
    But do you know what storks (and vultures) do?
    It's pretty neat.

Remember, bird DROPPINGS are often white instead of brown,
    and quite liquidy, and often POOPED upon the ground.
However, when a stork gets hot it squirts POOP on its legs,
    turning them from red or black to the color of its eggs.

And just like people's sweat, the liquid POOP evaporates,
    helping to cool off the storks so that they can feel great.
"Urohidrosis", or what this process now is termed,
    lowers the temperature of storks—it's been confirmed.

TORTOISES

Do you know the fable called *The Tortoise and the Hare?*
    "Slow and steady wins the race"
    is a message that's in there.
Watch how slowly tortoises walk
and how leisurely they graze,
    unhurriedly they DEFECATE—
    maybe once every couple of days.

Fruit-eating tortoises POOP seeds on tropical ground
    and in so doing, they plant some fruit trees all around.
Many other animals dispense fruit seeds like that:
    some tropical fish and "flying fox" (the large fruit bat).

The tortoise and the turtle have become popular pets.
    While turtles thrive in water,
    most tortoises are seldom wet.
However, they say it is good
for a tortoise to bathe each week
    to prevent dehydration
    (a constipation-easing technique!)

The turtle has webbed feet on its
back legs, to swim around;
    the tortoise uses stumpy feet
    for walking on the ground.
However, both are reptiles, so
some traits they share for sure,
    like using a cloaca
    (it's the Latin word for "sewer").

Umbrella Cockatoos

People use umbrellas to block rain or too much sun;
    umbrella cockatoos raise theirs in defense or for fun.
A large white parrot native to the tropical rainforests
    of Indonesia, this bird has quite a massive white crest.

They eat a diet, like most birds,
of fruit and nuts and seeds.
    When nesting, they eat insects, larvae—
    more protein they need.
And like other birds and reptiles,
the cloaca is present.
    Although, in birds, this opening
    is often called the "vent".

Unlike tortoises, cockatoos have
metabolisms quite high:
    they POOP two to three hours
    after eating and before they fly.
Because of such bowel timing,
they can be potty-trained as a pet.
    Being parrots, they might say "POO", too,
    when making their newspapers wet!

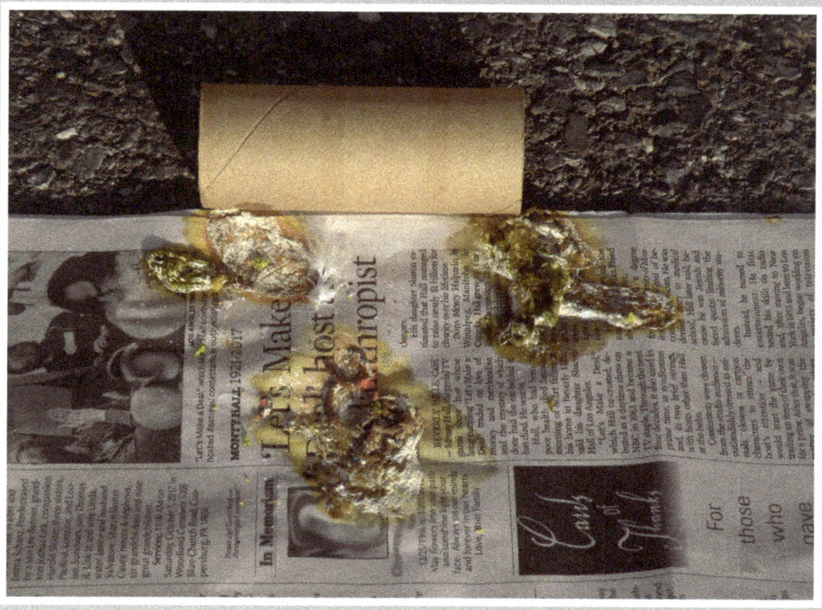
MONTY HALL 1921-2017
In Memoriam
For
those
who

Vietnamese Potbelly Pigs

From time to time a brave person will get
    a potbelly pig for a family pet.
Like a cat, a pig can be housebroken: taught
    to GO in a litter box when it ought.

To "eat like a pig" means to eat often, and much.
    They eat plants and animals (insects, worms, and such).
One of nature's vacuum cleaners, omnivorous swine
    are scavengers, like vultures and sharks, who like to dine

on just about anything, living or dead.
    Yet they're the cleanest farm animal, it's said!
An adult pig can POOP over 10 pounds per day—
    that's a lot of "PIG BERRIES" to compost with hay.

In their native country, these hungry potbelly pigs
    eat aquatic vegetation—they graze, root, and dig—
and in so doing, they consume water from wet plants.
    They'd perhaps dehydrate if not for this sustenance.

WHITE-TAILED DEER

Hunters track deer in various ways:
    they look for indentations in which deer did lay,
they try to find trees that antlers did scratch,
    and if tracks are scarce, then perhaps there's a batch

of black rounded PELLETS on piles here and there.
    Better watch where you step in the forest—beware!
Like a cow, deer chew cud, "ruminating" their food.
    Their food digests finely and comes out quite shiny.

In summer, deer DROPPINGS are oft' large and wet
    due to the abundance of food deer can get.
Their SCAT really varies with various seasons.
    In winter, it's pellet-like—eating twigs is the reason.

When a baby deer's born, hungry predators could tell
    how to find where it's hiding by tracking the smell
of the pee and the POO. So here's what the does do:
    get rid of FECAL MATTER—they don't leave a clue.

While she nurses her fawn, four or more times per day,
    the doe puts her nose on
    the newborn's bottom to say,
"It is time to POOP and to pee" (that is the cue).
    Then the mom drinks fawn urine
    and eats DROPPINGS, too!

eXamine Yours

It's generally a good idea
   to look at your pee and your POO.
Take notice of the shape and color,
   for that is a wise thing to do.

And if you find need to describe it,
   just look at the "Bristol STOOL Chart".
It classifies seven types of BOWEL MOVEMENTS
   by using descriptions and visual art.

Remember, if there's something odd,
   then your mom or dad ought be informed.
(Although if you recently ate some red beets,
   the "outcome" might not be the norm!)

You probably POOP on a toilet—
   it's a private thing to do.
And when you were born you wore diapers,
   until at least the age of two.

Your ancestors, before the toilet,
   used an outhouse, for that was the rage.
And wiped their behinds not with T.P.,
   but a newspaper or catalogue page.

The outhouse, or "privy", or "earth closet",
    or "dunny" (as in Australia's found),
was more comfy than squatting in fields
    or aiming at holes in the ground.

And when they couldn't get to the latrine—
    perhaps too dark or stormy or cold—
they stayed indoors with a "chamber pot".
    No indoor plumbing in days of old!

But these days you probably have a toilet
    in a bathroom, restroom, lavatory, or "loo".
And if you want to sound fancy, you could call it
    the "powder room", "water closet", or "w.c.", too.

Contemplate, as you sit on the toilet,
    "the throne", "hopper", "john", or "the pot",
that while all people must "DO THEIR DUTY",
    not all people have what they ought.

Be aware that there are people, worldwide,
    who lack the sanitation they need.
That's why World Toilet Day has been founded
    on November 19th, yes indeed!

Zebras

Zebra are from Africa. A cousin of the horse,
    they eat a lot of grass and leaves—
    they're herbivores, of course.
Looking close at zebra POOP, if you investigate,
    you might see bits of grass or leaves
    the zebra lately ate.

And if you watch a zebra at a zoo (or Africa),
    you'll notice a long tail it wags like a big fly swatter.
But when it lifts its tail up and points it out behind,
    it's ready to unload some DUNG
    for you-guess-who to find.

The dung beetles! They roll the POOP,
these cleaner-uppers do.
    Unless, of course, some scientists
    pick up the zebra POO
to use the microbes from the WASTE
to break down cellulose
    in paper, to make biofuel
    for cars—how grandiose!

So someday, if your car can run on "eco-friendly" fuel
   that's cheap and readily produced—
   no need for oil's drill—
you'd have the African zebra to thank for its input
   of gut bacteria it leaves
   behind in its WASTE output.

Now we know animal POOP has a purpose.
　　We have learned that it's seldom simply WASTE,
whether the animal lets go in leisure
　　or expels its EXCREMENT fast, in haste.

Animal POOP provides shelter for insects to live;
　　marks territory (protection for penguins it gives);
incubates eggs; also gives ants, flies, mice extra food;
　　even cools off birds in summer so they can feel good.

Sometimes the POOP can help plant some new fruit trees,
　　repel mosquitoes or fertilize for free,
waterproof homes, PASS fermented coffee,
　　make tea or paper or fuel or jewelry!

Remember, if you see animal POOP,
　　it could contain germs and such.
Because of diseases that you could catch,
　　you'd better just look and not touch.

And now that you've finished this alphabet book,
     it's time to reread and take a second look.
Try to find in "ABC order" these words:
     synonyms for POOP (like HAWK CHALK and TURDS).

52 Synonyms for POOP used in this book, in alphabetical order:

BM
BOWEL
   MOVEMENTS
BROWN GOLD
CECOTROPE
CHIPS
COPROLITE
DEFECATE
DOG DIRT
DOO-DOO
DO THEIR DUTY
DROP(PINGS)
DUNG
EXCREMENT
EXCRETE
FECAL MATTER
FECAL SACS
FECES

FLOPS
FRASS
GO (TO THE LOO)
GUANO
HAWK CHALK
LAND MINE
MANURE
MARINE MUD
MEADOW MUFFIN
MECONIUM
MOVEMENT
NIGHT DROPPINGS
NUMBER TWO
PASS
PATTIES
PELLETS
PIES
PIG BERRIES

PLOPPINGS
POO
POOP BALL
POOP RINGS
ROAD APPLE
SAND CLOUD
SCAT
SLICE
SOIL
SPLAT
SPLATTER
SPLAY
SPRAINT
STOOLS
TURDS
WASTE
WORM CASTINGS

Use a different synonym
     each week for one whole year.
Impress your friends, confound your folks,
     with what you have learned here!

POOP PICTURE SOURCES

A alligator **COPROLITE** ordered from ebay; thanks to Tom
B bat **GUANO** on cellar door, courtesy of eave-hanging bats
C cat **POOP** from cat owners, brothers Nick and Chris Laird
D backyard **DOG DIRT** (suburban "**LAND MINES**")
E "POOPOOPAPER" purchased from Alternative Pulp & Paper Co. Ltd., Thailand
F parrotfish **EXCREMENT** sand from Oahu's Southeast Shore, Hanauma Bay, Hawaii; thanks to Mario Marcozzi
G -goose **DROPPINGS** found on an outdoor walk near the Grist Mill in Hellertown, PA
H horse **MANURE** from Ursula Merriman's horse, Porter
I "chong shi cha" from Wang Xuan Hanshan Tea House, China
J cow **PIE** from Farmer Jim and Barbara Pavlica
K Lehigh Valley Zoo
L round rabbit **PELLETS** and **CECOTROPE** from Panther Rabbit (our pet bunny)
M mouse **DROPPINGS** from an unwanted visitor this past winter
N Lehigh Valley Zoo
O Lehigh Valley Zoo
P Lehigh Valley Zoo
Q Squire 6, LLC (a family-owned farm in PA)
R Lehigh Valley Zoo
S Lehigh Valley Zoo

T Lehigh Valley Zoo
U Lehigh Valley Zoo
V Lehigh Valley Zoo
W deer **SCAT** found on an outdoor walk
X —
Y —
Z Lehigh Valley Zoo

POOP PHOTOGRAPHERS

Sarah—A, C, D, H, K, M, Q, S, V, Z
Bonnie—the other letters

All **POOPS** were photographed with an Olympus 10 megapixel SP-565UZ Digital Camera with 20x optical zoom lens.

Note: An empty toilet paper roll was strategically placed in each setting to show the relative size of the **POOP** in relation to this familiar bathroom object.

No toilet paper rolls were harmed in the making of this book.

ABOUT THE AUTHOR

Bonnie has a penchant for arranging things in alphabetical order. The author of the early elementary ABC book *What Do Animals Eat?*, she wanted to write a sequel aimed at late elementary school-aged kids—and here it is!

She played piano at a boutique bistro, cooked and managed a kitchen at a gourmet deli, and taught Algebra I in a "restorative practices" school, before becoming a published author.

Bonnie lives with her family in the Lehigh Valley, Pennsylvania, where she works as a church musician.

Believe it or not, her favorite color is brown.

ABOUT THE ASSISTANT PHOTOGRAPHER

Sarah loves reading books, especially Hellertown library books. When she helped take the pictures, she was in third grade. She took 10 of the pictures in this book.

Sarah likes animals, playing with stuffed animals, and Panther, her pet rabbit. Her favorite animal is a bunny.

Sarah enjoys dance and chorus. Her favorite TV shows are *Full House* and *The Middle*. Her three favorite foods are macaroni and cheese with tuna, tuna fish sandwiches, and pizza. She also likes making hats and bracelets out of yarn. Her favorite color is sky blue.

PROCEEDS

A portion of the revenue from the sales of this book will be donated to food-focused charities seeking to end childhood hunger in America.

—*Bonnie and Sarah*